Starting Over

JANICE AUSTIN

Copyright © 2014 Janice Austin
Print Edition

All rights reserved.

DEDICATION

To all of those women who have experienced significant changes in their lives and like the butterfly have set everything that was once known aside and embraced an entirely new way of being. In many ways the butterfly represents the human soul. It is the symbol of transition and change in your life.

CONTENTS

Dedication iii
Acknowledgements v
Preface vi
Chapter One 1
Chapter Two 5
Chapter Three 8
Chapter Four 12
Chapter Five 14
Chapter Six 17
Chapter Seven 19
Chapter Eight 24
Chapter Nine 26
Chapter Ten 28
Chapter Eleven 30
Chapter Twelve 32
Chapter Thirteen 34
Chapter Fourteen 37
Chapter Fifteen 39
Chapter Sixteen 41
Chapter Seventeen 44
Chapter Eighteen 46
Chapter Nineteen 50
Chapter Twenty 52
Chapter Twenty-One 54
Chapter Twenty-Two 60
Chapter Twenty-Three 62
Chapter Twenty-Four 64
Chapter Twenty-Five 66
Chapter Twenty-Six 68
Photographs 73
About the Author 78

ACKNOWLEDGEMENTS

To Paula Clancy for her beautiful cover and to Brad Justice for helping edit and format! You are both so special!

PREFACE

My love for books started early in my maternal grandfather's library. I was so impressed that someone had a room with nothing but bookcases and books. My maternal grandfather was a real Renaissance Man, a gentleman, and a scholar. A principal of a high school, he taught mathematics for fifty years. He also published a book of poetry and was sought after by mathematicians from across the country as a master problem solver. I credit him with sharing his love of books with me. His calm and quiet presence was very important in my young life. I always felt safe and happy while in his library. Later on when reading *To Kill a Mockingbird* and later seeing the movie, I associated the role of Atticus, played by Gregory Peck, with my papa. So, growing up, books became a big part of my world. They were someplace to escape into a secret world, travel to many countries, and find interesting new friends.

Books continue today to be a major influence in my life. You can have all of the Kindles in the world, but nothing is so magical and personal as the feel of turning pages in a real bound book, seeing what will happen next. This love of reading has inspired me to write my story. "Starting Over" is a journey of struggle, self-doubt, discovery, and acceptance that I would not want to do over, but would not have wanted to miss.

To fully tell my story, I need to start with how it all began…

CHAPTER ONE

I moved a lot in my early childhood. My dad was a brilliant engineer and usually had a good job. One was as an engineer in Oak Ridge, Tennessee, during the creation of the Atom bomb. Although we now see how this changed the course of history, at that early age, I did not grasp the significance of that epic fact. Unfortunately, my dad was also a gambler and an alcoholic, which did not make for a "Leave It to Beaver" home environment. We were in and out of money, but fortunately, my mother could stretch a dollar until it squealed. Therefore, we never went hungry or homeless.

Poor Dad was somewhat of a pitiful victim, having been raised by parents who worshiped him, along with his nine older sisters. They bought him a car when he was fourteen years old, which he immediately wrecked. He collected money from his sisters regularly just by attending school each day. As a young adult, he passed a Civil Engineering test without ever attending college. Although smart and jovial, he was totally irresponsible.

My mother, on the other hand, was a rock but very passive and introverted. Although rarely showing emotion, she was a very loving parent who would do anything for her children. I had a younger brother who we all adored, and still do to this day.

Due to my dad's "bad behavior" and my mother's "quiet resistance," I found myself thrust into a "parental role." I was the only one who could control my dad when he was on one of his binges. At an early age, I would tell him to go to bed when he was acting wildly, and much to my surprise, he obeyed. I remember being a very young child and picking up a shoe to threaten him if he did not do that. Surprisingly, it seemed to work. One day, he told my uncle with a sense of pride that "No one would ever walk all over me." Little did he know.

My mother had been a teacher before marriage, becoming a stay-at-home mom afterwards. She read to me constantly from an early age. Therefore, I skipped kindergarten and first grade, being sent directly to second grade. In those days, there were no accelerated classrooms, so skipping was very common. This was in Birmingham, Alabama, a town that was full of civil rights issues. I remember riding the bus when only white people were allowed to sit. I also remember not understanding why white and black people could not eat together, or even drink out of the same water fountains. It did not seem fair in my young mind, but I knew not to ask too many questions. It was not dinnertime conversation.

During this time, I remember a little girl in my class who did not appear to have many clothes. Wanting to help, I went home, packed up a big sack of mine, and took them to school the next day. My mother found out and put an end to that. After all, we certainly did not have a good deal of money. So, that was the end of my philanthropy. Maybe this was an omen for the social work career to come?

I went to third and fourth grades in Knoxville, Tennessee. I kept a diary in those days, which portrayed a little girl, wise beyond her years, being the family peacemaker. I kept journals a lot in my life and now know that it was a great coping device. My feelings were always safe there. My brother was more passive, like my mother, and he was pretty much left alone. He basically did his own "thing," never got into trouble, and was left to hang out with friends a great deal of the time.

CHAPTER TWO

We moved to Louisville, Kentucky, at the beginning of my seventh grade year. I was so tired of being the new girl in school and having to prove myself. However, I credit my push to be known and recognized to that period of my life. I always tried out for everything, and usually got it. In junior high, I was on the yearbook staff and student council, while serving as class representative, and even had a major role in the school operetta. I also always had a lot of friends, which looking back was my haven, since the at-home situation was so chaotic. I usually would not invite any friends to my home because I never knew what the situation would be like. I remember one time bringing a friend home and discovered my dad, unclothed and drunk, on the living room couch. I was humiliated and said to myself, "Never again would I expose myself to the ridicule that I felt."

I started Louisville Girls High School in 1950.

There was no coeducation in Louisville at that time. We marched to class, wore uniforms, and it was a very academic atmosphere. I even had poetry published in the school newspaper. I joined a very elite but snobby sorority and thrived under the structured environment.

In 1951, coeducation came to Louisville and changed my world. Boys, sports, and cheerleading became my focus. Being one of the first cheerleaders at Manual High School was a major coup. I was also "in love" or maybe "in like" with one of the basketball players and president of the senior class. My grades suffered, but it was a lot of fun! I remember the annual Thanksgiving Game (Male-Manual) and how excited we were. We would be on local television (black and white) for making Louisville history. I had been practicing my cartwheel for weeks in anticipation of this event, and guess who fell flat on her backside on TV that day? I also remember on this day telling my mother that all of the cheerleaders would be entering the field with mouton coats over their uniforms and that I would be the only member without one. My dear, sweet mother brought out of the attic a mouton coat that she had been saving for Christmas. Yes, I was a drama queen.

I might add that I had a "clothes fetish" even then. Mother would work part-time at Stewart Department Store to buy me clothes and would also make a lot of them. I remember my Class Day dress-blue voile and a work of art. I would also work after school at Stewarts Dry Goods, stuffing envelopes to buy my prom dresses. A sense of style was always something that I prided myself with possessing. I always wanted good clothes, even if they were few. A couple of cashmere sweaters, crisp white blouses, and a good basic black dress and suit were my standbys. I discovered that with accessories, a new look could be established and therefore become a fashion statement. Somehow, I was voted best dressed in high school. That was an amazing achievement. A lot of the credit went to my mother who would copy fashions seen in the department stores.

CHAPTER THREE

I was only sixteen when I first arrived on campus at the University of Kentucky. My roommates were best friends from high school. We were away from home for the first time and very excited at our newfound freedom.

Inexperienced in the ways of the world, we were introduced to the exciting evils of alcohol and cigarettes. Samples of cigarettes were given out at freshman orientation. We had never smoked, except at camp or slumber parties, when immediately after, we would experience the most horrible effects. As far as drinking, it was only experimental.

I was a whopping ninety pounds and one Planters Punch would put me under. I was really a cheap drunk. Memories of being on the top bunk and seeing the ceiling spin stay with me. I recently talked to my former roommate and we reminisced about our attempts at being cool. I was always aware of the genetic danger of alcoholism that ran in my family, and quickly discovered that I did not like to drink enough to feel not in control.

We were all three virgins, attractive, and had many dates. In those days, "going all the way" was out of the question, and getting pregnant was not going to happen. Remember, those were the days before birth control. We did not want to have a "bad reputation." Only "loose" women had sex before marriage. So, we were often called "big teases" by our dates. One of my dates was Dan Chandler, son of Governor Happy Chandler. We double dated with a friend of mine and John Y. Brown, whose main claim to fame at the time was selling the most encyclopedias on campus.

My friend and I planned to try out for cheerleading. This was in the day before gymnastics was a necessity. We had been teammates for a big city school and thought our chances were good. Unfortunately, on the day of tryouts, I had a flu bug and had to go home. She made the squad. Being a University of Kentucky cheerleader was not going to happen for me and I remember being so disappointed.

Unfortunately, after one and a half years, my father died and I had to return home, leaving school. There was not much money and it was understood to be much more important for my brother to have a college degree. After all, I was expected to marry well, have a family, and be supported by my husband. It did not seem fair, but that was just the way people thought in those days. My major was elementary education and I really did not want to teach. So perhaps getting a job, having a car, and having some money to spend was not so bad.

I was always cognizant of money issues that existed with my mother raising a young teenager alone, so I paid rent and gave my brother an allowance. Mother was an amazing woman, getting a job as a bookkeeper at General Electric, and learning to drive in her mid forties. However, she really never learned to park properly and took the driving test three times. I will always remember her little white Falcon and her pride in being able to drive it to work every day. She was in pain, even then, as rheumatoid arthritis took its toll on her body. While hardly ever complaining, suffering in silence was her badge of honor.

Communication was always an issue with my mother because she never liked to talk about personal problems. She would say, "You never air your dirty laundry in public." So, I never knew how she felt about my dad's death because it simply was not discussed. I carried a lot of anger towards him for what I thought was just plain weakness of character. I did not realize what a disease alcoholism was. Before his death, he stayed sober for almost two years before going on a binge with his fishing buddies. I did not realize the impact of the disease and thought he should have had better control. For years, I also did not discuss him with anyone. It was though I had erased his existence, but of course it was buried deep in me.

CHAPTER FOUR

I wanted to be an airline stewardess. During the 1950s, it was considered to be the most glamorous career that a young girl could have. So, when I saw an ad in the Louisville newspaper, I jumped at the chance to have an interview. Making sure my hair, nails, and outfit were as perfect as could be, I proceeded to meet a representative from TWA at a local hotel.

I passed! I was told that I would be getting a letter from TWA informing me of training school details, to be held in Kansas City, Missouri. What excitement! I could hardly contain myself as I hurried home to tell my mother the good news. However, I don't think she shared my degree of enthusiasm.

I arrived in Kansas City with a group of other girls from all over the country. It would have been close to a beauty pageant of today. They interviewed us, weighed us, measured us, etc. I was very petite, barely 5'1", and ninety pounds, so I was stretching their standards. I remember drinking milkshakes and stuffing myself, trying to gain a few pounds, but to no avail. After two weeks, I was sadly sent home. My glamorous airline stewardess career had a short life. I think that I was mostly upset because I would not get to wear that cute uniform. I am also not so sure that I was ready to leave the nest. My mother and younger brother were an important part of my life and I felt protective of their well-being. It was not meant to be! I settled back into life in Louisville, went out with President of the Bachelors Club, met a cute officer at Fort Knox that was actually a cadet at West Point, traveled to New York for a dance at the Point and was enjoying my singledom!

CHAPTER FIVE

In 1954, the primary career paths for young women were as nurses, teachers, or secretaries. Since I had not completed my college degree, I went the secretary route. My first job experience was as a receptionist for the famed Louisville Orchestra. Robert Whitney was the esteemed director and we had many famous artists from all over the world coming to Louisville. One that I remember in particular was Van Cliburn, the wonderful pianist. That was a fun, exciting time for a young eighteen year old. I stayed there for about a year until I heard about an opportunity at a family-owned distillery, Stitzel Weller. They were looking for a secretary with advertising experience. I proceeded to go to the library and check out every book that I could find related to advertising and marketing, so I could wow them during my interview. It worked! I got the job.

Pappy Van Winkle had been in the bourbon business for many years, starting out as a salesman. Everyone who knew him, loved him. At the time of my employment, he was in his eighties, but his presence was very much there. Quite the colorful character, he would roam the surrounding woods around the area in his camouflage suit, blasting away at some poor dove or quail. His dogs usually accompanied him on these walks. Julian Jr. was in charge at this time, but Pappy still kept an office complete with his spittoon, necessary for all of his cigar-smoking and spitting.

This was a wonderful working experience. As you turned onto Limestone Lane past ivy-covered columns, there were tall oak trees leading to the warehouses and picturesque red-bricked office building with a white pillared portico. The pungent smell of bourbon would envelope you. I remember having a toothache and the master distiller taking me to the warehouse for a dose of Old Fitzgerald.

I learned advertising/marketing tips and strategies that I use even today. We advertised in all of the national magazines, and for years, I received complimentary issues of *Time*, *Life*, and *Newsweek*, no matter where I lived. All in all, a good education!

And, try buying Pappy Van Winkle bourbon today. You will wait in line for some time, as it is made in very small quantities.

I stayed at this job until after I was married and

pregnant with my first child. I became very ill, was hospitalized and told that I needed bed rest, so I had to quit. We then had to move in with my mother and brother until student housing became available. After all, I had been the breadwinner. As an intern, my husband's salary was a whopping $65 a month. But, I am getting ahead of myself.

CHAPTER SIX

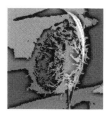

Life in the 1950s was so different than today. We did not know the world of drugs and no one locked their doors. Children played outside until dark. Our neighborhood was a close-knit one. Although we did not have a lot of money, no one who we knew did, either. We lived in a neighborhood of small homes with manicured lawns and neighbors looking after neighbors. So in many ways, it was good and we enjoyed years of innocence.

But, in many ways, the 1950s were the beginning of a different radical world. Introduced were Rock 'n' Roll and the Civil Rights Movement. However, premarital sex was still taboo. Girls who became in a "family way" were often shipped off to live with relatives or to a home for pregnant girls.

Major moral attitudes were intact and life seemed simpler. I was definitely a product of those times. That was my safe comfortable familiar world!

CHAPTER SEVEN

I married in 1957. I was twenty-two years old and most of my friends had already walked down the aisle. My husband-to-be was twenty-five and doing an internship at Louisville Children's Hospital. We had met on a blind date because my cousin was in his class. I guess timing had a lot to do with the courtship and impending wedding. He was a suitable candidate, a doctor-to-be, and there was some charisma, so it seemed the thing to do. We were engaged for a year, but part of that time was spent apart, as he was out of town working with a medical practice in western Kentucky. So, I am not sure that we knew each other as well as most engaged couples do today. Yes, as a product of the 1950s, I was a virgin. Actually, he was too. I have often wondered if that was a good thing. He made up for the lack of experimentation later in our marriage with other women.

I paid for my beautiful wedding dress, which cost $500, a monumental price in those days. The reception was held at a Woman's Club in Louisville. It was a beautiful Christmas-themed wedding and everything seemed to go smoothly. We left the reception for a honeymoon in New Orleans. I was very excited to start a new life and visit this historic city. One of the salesmen from my workplace was a native of New Orleans and got us reservations at the famed Roosevelt Hotel and at some famous restaurants. We were both nervous about this new journey and I have to share a funny story: When my new husband opened the closet in our hotel room, there was a mirror. He saw himself and screamed. I laughed until I cried and that helped put us both at ease.

Things were so different sexually in those days. Now, we see experimentation before marriage and some even choose not to marry and live together.

Soon after the wedding, I became pregnant with our oldest child. It was also soon after when I discovered that I had married an immature "mama's boy." We were in need of a new washer/dryer, but before completing the transaction, had to get permission from Mama.

During the pregnancy, he was gone thirty-six hours and home for twelve. Without any money or transportation, I found myself alone in a small "student housing" apartment. I might add that we did not have air conditioning, except for a small window unit in the bedroom. In order to keep the air cool in the room, he rigged up a cardboard door, which you had to crawl through, from the small space at the bottom. This was my world, and shortly after the birth of this child, I found myself pregnant once again. With a newborn and a seventeen month old, even though I loved my babies, I was very busy, very tired, very alone, and very stressed. One of the most irritating things that I remember was when my spouse came home after hours at the hospital, rubbing his fingers along the top of furniture to see if there was any dust. Needless to say, it was not an endearing act. I think this had a' lot to do with the fact that his mother had a cleaning fetish and he grew up with plastic covering all of their living room furniture. I soon felt like I was trapped into a situation and there was no way out.

After all, no one in that time divorced with two small children. I decided to "make the best of it," but seriously knew that I was no longer in love with this person and hoped that I could regain those romantic feelings. The old saying then was, "If you make your bed, you simply sleep in it." I thought that things would improve as our financial condition got better. Later, I discovered the hard way that money certainly does not bring happiness.

There never was a question of where we would live after he completed the internship – his hometown. My experience up to that point was that people would question any and every aspect of your life in this small town. His mother gave us a welcoming tea at the Woman's Club. I was expected to know every guest's name and what they had given as a wedding gift as they came through the receiving line. Also, the wife of his old high school buddy had told me that because I was a doctor's wife, I would need to be aware of my appearance, even while shopping at the grocery. I was also told by my mother-in-law not to tell anyone that I was not a college graduate or that I had worked in a place that made whiskey. It was all scary, but eager to have a house, more space, a yard, air conditioning, and to be able to afford a few luxuries, I welcomed the move. After all, I would be leaving that tiny apartment with its cardboard door to the bedroom.

My oldest was two and the baby was six months when we moved into a wonderful and picturesque home. I remember having an income of $60,000 a year, which seemed a fortune. It was 1960 and I felt on top of the world. I was able to make new friends, have some help with the children, and was very content with my Norman Rockwell life.

CHAPTER EIGHT

In 1963, I discovered that I was pregnant with twins. It was exciting and I felt extremely important and proud of myself. Life was good. However, that was the beginning of hearing rumors about my husband's infidelity, which I dismissed. I told myself that those things did not happen in my life, but my suspicions were at times aroused. The person in question was a nurse in his office who babysat for us on a regular basis. It could not be, I would say to myself. However, I often found myself wondering why he was so late getting home from giving her a ride, after she sat for the children. It did play games with my mind. One night after taking her home, he asked what I thought about adopting her little girl. Imagine, I had two babies under four, twins on the way, and was asked this crazy question. I was furious and told him that he was crazy. That ended the strange conversation. Nothing else was ever mentioned, however, I never forgot the awkwardness and strangeness. We were neither good at expressing feelings, so, I began to bury mine. I preferred being in denial.

CHAPTER NINE

When the twins were eighteen months old, my husband was drafted in the Vietnam War Doctor Draft and sent to basic training. I was left alone with four small children to sell the house and pack up everything for the impending move to Fort Hood, Texas. During training, my husband was very distant and said that he was very sick, so there was not a lot of interaction. This appeared very odd, but I think that I was just so busy and did not let my mind go there. Looking back, I believe that he was lovesick because he had left his girlfriend.

The two years spent at Fort Hood were probably the happiest of our entire marriage. We had a carefree attitude and the children seemed happy with having their dad home more. We met new and exciting people from all over the country and pursued fun activities as a family. I learned to ride a horse, the older children were on the Fort Hood Dolphins swim team, and my oldest son loved cub scouts. My daughter took ballet lessons and the twins were enrolled in daycare on the post, of which I served on the board. It was a busy, but grand time.

After the two years were coming to a close, I begged him to consider staying in the military, or at least look at practice someplace other than in the town where we had lived before, but to no avail. Looking back, I know that I had a premonition that things would not be good if we returned. I really never had a choice. It was as if he would not be able to survive anyplace else. Being a big fish in a small pond was so important to his ego.

CHAPTER TEN

The year is 1968 and we are building "the grand house." It will have five bedrooms, living room, dining room, family room, study, breakfast room, kitchen, mudroom, four full baths, two half-baths, and another kitchen in the unfinished basement. What a glorious time I had picking out wall colors, carpet, tile, appliances, wall paper, etc. The focal point of the home will be the foyer with its black slate floor and black wrought iron circular stairway. We had traveled to Atlanta to view a replica and one that had been featured in *Parents Magazine*. It had giant columns in front with stained glass windows on either side of the massive door, bought from a church in Atlanta. Our architect was a local man who brought master craftsman carpenters with him. The dining room cupboard and other built-in features were works of art.

This massive house sat on a lot surrounded by eleven acres of woods. As it was being built, local nosies would drive up, get out, walk around, and discuss its dimensions. Funny! One person asked if it were going to be a library.

CHAPTER ELEVEN

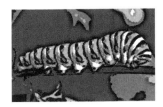

I had a beautiful family. The twins were four and the older two were eight and nine years old. My husband resumed his medical practice and was soon very busy with his patients and with being a good family man. I remember thinking to myself, "I have a beautiful, perfect life." We belonged to a country club, had a great social life, the children were doing well in school, and I was starting to get involved in community activities. I also had wonderful friends.

Soon, things began to change. It was a "party scene." We began to hear about "free love" and "if it feels good, do it." Our social network was made up of college faculty, other physicians, local businessmen, and their wives. It started out so innocent. We would congregate at each other's houses on the weekend and there would be a lot of drinking, dancing, and flirting. Even though for most of us it ended there, the seeds of temptation were let loose. We began to hear about men we knew having affairs, faculty with students, and physicians with nurses and patients. It was as if the dams were let loose for many, and morality took a nose dive. Our children were beginning to experiment with drugs and it was a very frightening time in our culture. Most of us did not understand what dangers were out there. Alcohol remained the drug of choice for my generation.

CHAPTER TWELVE

Cooking and entertainment were never a chore for me. I loved to play hostess every chance that I got. Small dinner parties were my favorite, but I have had as many as two hundred in my home for a Murray State Homecoming Buffet.

One of my most memorable guests was Dr. Benjamin Spock. He was in town to address students of the University on the evils of the Vietnam War. That was a very controversial subject in the conservative town of Murray, Kentucky. Actually, one of our closest friends, a boy scout leader and huge patriotic flag waver, refused to attend.

Dr. Spock had just written his book on twins, which made his visit even more relevant to me, since my twins were toddlers at the time. He was a gracious guest, and I treasured his thank you note that complimented me on my menu of beaten biscuits and ham, fresh asparagus, fruit salad, and derby pie.

The reason that I had the good fortune of having Dr. Spock as a dinner guest was because of a friend of mine, who was in charge of providing speakers at the University. Also, my husband was the only pediatrician in town.

Another guest was Ashley Montagu, who had been a guest several times on Johnny Carson's show. An anthropologist and author, he was also somewhat of a controversial figure in his time.

I remember trying Oysters Rockefeller for the first time and trying to be sophisticated.

Someone once called me the Perle Mesta of Murray. She was a famous Texas hostess, so I was flattered. This is a part of the journey that makes me smile and feel validated.

CHAPTER THIRTEEN

The so-called sexual revolution was considered by many to be the most shocking social trend in the 1970s. The sexual revolution, an outgrowth of the counterculture, cast aside traditional sexual restraints and began a decade of alternative eroticism, experimentation, and promiscuity. In part facilitated by the development of the birth-control pill and other contraceptives, Americans in the 1970s broke many sexual taboos. Interracial dating, open homosexuality, communal living, casual nudity, and dirty language all seemed to indicate a profound change in sexual behavior. Sexual activity among the young especially increased. Surveys during the 1970s reported that by age nineteen, four-fifths of all males and two-thirds of all females had had sex. Fashion designers promoted a new sensuality, producing miniskirts, hot pants, halter tops, and formfitting clothes designed to accentuate women's sexuality.

Source: American Decades, ©*2000 Gale Cengage. All Rights Reserved.*

You always think it will never happen to you. Nothing can burst that little bubble you have created. Then one day, after wondering why things had changed so dramatically in my marital relationship, I found the tape. It was a lovesick verbal pile of garbage to a patient of his with whom he was engaged in an extramarital affair. On the tape, he professes undying love and that he wants to spend the rest of his life with her. He also says about me, "I wish she were dead." That was probably the most hurtful thing that had ever happened to me. I was devastated. Of course, it explained his inattention, verbal abuse, unexplained absences, and all, but that was no consolation. I went to bed and stayed there for two days until a good friend came to visit, made a pitcher of Bloody Mary's, and we laughed ourselves goofy. I will always be grateful to my good friend for forcing me back into the world of sanity.

I continued to feel such pain and hurt. The words on the tape haunted me. I found out that on one of our recent trips to visit my mother in Louisville, he had left our twin boys in a motel by themselves, and drove to Hodgenville to meet his lover. The twins were only five years old at the time.

I had stayed with the two older children and Mother in her small apartment. By putting the boys in danger, it clearly told me that he was "off his rocker." Were we in danger, should I feel fearful?

I filed for divorce thinking I could no longer live with this man. But, he said he did not want a divorce. He claimed to have broken it off with his girlfriend, so we arranged to go to Nashville to a marriage counselor.

He, however, did not stop seeing her. Everything he told me and the marriage counselor were lies and what he thought we needed to hear. I also found out that he was paying this woman's tuition to medical school in Louisville, long after he claimed it had ended. Pretty ironic, when later in life, he did not contribute to his children's college educations.

Probably due in part to his persuasion and my fear, I decided to ride it out. He claimed to have ended the affair and wanted to make a go of the marriage.

This was in 1972.

Of course, it did not end. He went to someone else, a student nurse rotating through his office. This is a whole new chapter in this sorry saga!

CHAPTER FOURTEEN

Looking back again………

I was in thirty-six years old, my husband was having a love affair, I had a bleeding cyst, and had to have a sudden partial hysterectomy. What more could happen? I remember him coming to the hospital, showing complete indifference towards me, and fussing about my oldest son's report card. Whatever he could come up with to cause distress, make me feel bad about myself, and place blame, he did.

Later, I discovered that he had entertained his girlfriend in my home and in our bed. Like I said, whatever he could do to justify his guilt, he would do. Good example: After returning home from the hospital, partly because I had lost weight and mostly because I also needed a shopping "high," I visited my favorite shop. I gathered up items to take home and try on, when suddenly, one of the owners asked me to come to the backroom. She hesitantly and with great embarrassment said that my husband had called, telling them not to let me charge anything and that he would no longer pay my bills. Shock, humiliation, grief, and total shame hit me with such a blow. I burst into tears and said how sorry I was to put her in such a situation. She insisted that I take the clothes home and in my stupefied state, did so. I went with the clothing to my friend's house and completely broke down. I begged my friend to take them back for me and that I was too ashamed to go back in the shop. What a cowardly act from that man. What else was there in store for me? I totally lost all trust, respect, and love, feeling like I was living with a coldhearted stranger. But, I felt trapped. I had four children, financial security, and a lifestyle. How could I support myself and my family if I left him? Did I continue to prostitute myself for security? I remained wounded until the day I finally got the courage to ask for a divorce, four years later. Any respect of this person was totally gone and I knew this was the end.

CHAPTER FIFTEEN

I could not even utter her name without shuddering. What an impact this young girl was to have on my children and myself. She claims to have been only nineteen when she first was with my husband (at least two years earlier than I had originally known about). Rotating through his office as a student nurse from MSU with an infant child, she had long brown hair, big hips, and that earthy, hippie look, popular in that period. The first time I saw her, she had on cutoff jean shorts and a loose shirt. I would have never taken her for the femme fatale she turned out to be.

He woke me up in the middle of the night saying he wanted a separation. Not a divorce, but a separation, mind you. I asked if there was someone else and he lied, saying no. I sobbed, but said, "Okay, get out in the morning but before you leave, you tell the children that you are leaving and the reason why." The twins were upset, but not the two older children. They had seen and heard too much in the past. In fact, they seemed relieved to not have to listen to the arguments anymore.

It wasn't long before he moved into a duplex with his paramour. My son reacted to this by taking him a housewarming present. He dumped his medical books in the middle of the yard and put a dead raccoon on top. Funny now, but so sad for him to feel it necessary to express his anger and disgust in this way.

In December of that year, the two of them married. He was forty-four and she was twenty-two.

My daughter actually overheard a conversation between him and this person over our intercom system. Evidently, it was a very vulgar conversation and one that you would not want your child to overhear. So, I think they were tired of the whole scene at that point. My oldest son used to follow him in the evenings and tell me where he was. This, I did not initiate. But it was extremely sad that he felt a need for this action.

CHAPTER SIXTEEN

My divorce decree seemed fair, but in my naiveté, I must confess that I was not one to know or say. In his haste to get things going, he agreed to share an attorney. I admit that was one of my first big mistakes. Another one of the biggest was not knowing there was very little equity in the house. That proved to be the start of my financial doom. However, looking back, it really did not matter what was in the decree because it was never enforced in the courts of the town where we lived.

Divorce, such an ugly happening, and one that we had not witnessed a lot until the 1970s. I thought it would never be part of my world, not in a million years. But, I really should not have been so surprised when he left. After all, there had been no real communication, warmth, affection, or sex for some time. I also was experiencing a lot of verbal abuse. He was constantly finding fault with me and the children, generally making everyone feel bad. I remember one day, he said, "You would never make it in the real world." Those words later came back to haunt me.

I had to do a lot of soul searching. Was I to blame? I felt rejection and shame. I knew I had not given him the affection and attention that he needed and craved. I was never able to recover from the betrayal, losing respect and trust. With that went any love I might have ever had. So, I did blame myself, too.

I have a history of using shopping as therapy to make myself feel less anxious and sad. He was able to use that as a criticism, a lot. Of course, he neglected to talk about all of his bad business deals. He once bought $40,000 of land in Texas, that did not exist, from a smooth talking scam artist who hit town. Several other doctors in town also got taken. That was one of many reckless decisions. We were both really a mess.

I know things are never completely one-sided, so I am sure that I played a role in the separation. I simply did not fulfill him, and I knew it. My self-worth was greatly diminished. Would anyone ever want me?

My anger was wild and stormy. At times, I felt like I could kill him, and understand how crimes of passion could occur. One of my friends came to the house one night when I said that I thought I might stab him with a pair of scissors. I don't know if I would have been that crazy, but the thoughts ran rampant and out of control.

Divorce became more common, but for some, it was still a real stigma of shame. One of my older aunts reportedly said about me, "Well, she might as well be dead." I think I was the first in my family to become a divorced woman.

CHAPTER SEVENTEEN

My big, beautiful home was on the market for sale. I had made the decision to move to Lexington. The twins were beginning high school, so it had to be now, or wait three more years. Unfortunately, in my naïve and uninformed state, I thought there was more equity in the home. After all, I thought that was why I had an attorney. The night before the closing, after everything was being packed and ready for movers, I was told that my ex had put a lien on the house when he purchased a local garden center. Therefore, a great deal of the equity was tied up. Not only did I feel stupid for not knowing, but also disbelief, that someone I had lived with for almost twenty years could have done this to me. I felt like I had to go ahead with the closing, but the banker convinced me that the money could be put into a CD and held by the bank for a period of time. He also led me to believe that it would be a safe transaction. My attorney had my ex sign an agreement that if anything happened to the money, he would make it good. Yeah, sure. About a year after leaving, the garden center took bankruptcy and there went my money. Now, the next thing would be to make sure the ex made good on his agreement, right? Easier said than done. Years later, after trying to collect on child support, alimony, and this agreement, although he was in contempt of court, the courts were not very effective. After all, the judge had been personal friends with his father and it was very much a good old boys school of thought. I later, finally, settled in desperation for $15,000, which was a fraction of the original amount. I also found out that he had not been making payments, which was part of our divorce agreement, so that was also taken out of the proceeds. I left town with a whopping $20,000 equity from this huge home.

So, I traded a 7600 square foot house with five bedrooms and five and a half baths for a small condo with three bedrooms in an apartment community in Lexington. I grieved for that house, and for many years would dream of being back there, only to wake up in a cold sweat, back to my reality.

CHAPTER EIGHTEEN

Suddenly the fear engulfed me like the most ominous black cloud on a stormy April day. I am penniless, with four children, two in college and two starting high school. I had no job skills, college degree, or influential contacts in the workforce. I had few friends and Lexington had changed since the 1950s, a lot. I would not even have had a home, but for my mother. She and my aunt provided the down payment with the idea that Mother would move in with us. She was very ill with rheumatoid arthritis and in an extreme amount of constant pain. I would lie in my bedroom at night, hearing her moan and cry in her sleep. That would set me off and I would do the same, but quietly.

My mother was very stoic with her suffering. She always kept her feelings and emotions to herself. Even though I knew she was miserable, she tried not to show it. I, in turn, did the same with the children. It was as though I was in denial, or perhaps, being protective. Anyway, I did not divulge my feelings of misery. One of my twins came home one day, saw me crying and said, "Mom, we moved to Lexington so you could be happy." I knew that they had left a familiar and comfortable environment, where they had grown up with their friends. I felt guilty that I had taken them away. It was their first day in high school, where they knew no one. They other twin said, "I had my last class of the day with my brother, and I was even glad to see him." That really hit home! I missed my good friends and made way too many long distance calls at night. I also missed my grand home. I would say to myself, especially when having a pity party at night, "I want my life back." On some evenings, I would even hit the bottle and then feel even worse the next day. I also knew that I had to be in control of my life and that this did not help.

A friend of mine called, saying that she had spoken to my ex's bride. The wife had threatened to leave if he sent any more money to Lexington, so all support had ended. When I questioned him and said that I would have to go back to court, I received letters with sharp knives and daggers all over the pages. Weird behavior, but disturbing.

I kept our poverty as hidden as I could from the children, but looking back, that was probably a mistake. After all, tennis strings and speech team trips took a lot of money. At one point, I worked three jobs. I might add that the boys had afterschool jobs, also. We were barely surviving and certainly not living the way in which we had been accustomed.

No money. Four teenagers. I needed to sell some things. I began with some pieces of furniture, a couple of rugs, and progressed to silver items and then my wedding diamond. Going back to court any more was futile. After all, as one judge said, "We can't put the good doctor in jail. He is our pediatrician." Besides, if I were to get anything, I would have to give forty percent to the lawyers. At this time, I had been through three sets of attorneys and two judges. I decided that I just had to get on with my life, put on a "happy face" for my family, and try to survive.

Mother had entered a nursing home and was terribly unhappy. Visiting and seeing her this way increased my sense of desperation. I now know that I was suffering from untreated depression. I didn't know coping strategies and there were no support groups or counseling services available. I guess my saving grace was my ability to find some sort of deprecating humor in my demise. That and my occasional vodka episodes, which left me feeling even more helpless and fearful. I derived strength from my four intelligent and aspiring children.

CHAPTER NINETEEN

My daughter was getting married. It was 1982, my mother was in the nursing home, and the twins were leaving for college (one to Vanderbilt and the other to Dennison). Thank God for scholarships, student loans, work-study, and even Pell Grants, as no money for college was forthcoming from their father. I didn't know how we could possibly pay for the wedding, but creatively, we came up with resources. I was able to borrow $1,000 from the bank, she wore my wedding gown, the clubhouse at the Oaks was lovely and affordable, and all of my new friends provided wonderful food. My musician son-in-law used his contacts to provide a trio of fellow musicians and my daughter's best friend was her Maid of Honor. So, it became a small and intimate, but lovely event.

She asked her father to give her away. I was so hoping, that by this gesture, he would offer to help with expenses. But no, he offered a plate of ham for the reception. Unbelievable... not even country ham. After the reception, my ex-sister-in-law offered to help, writing a check for $25.00. I graciously accepted her generous contribution. I guess it runs in the family.

My son-in-law's mother paid for their honeymoon to the Smokey Mountains and the happy couple took off for a new life together. I couldn't believe that we pulled it off.

CHAPTER TWENTY

My mother-in-law was very supportive of my situation. Although she suffered from an extreme dose of family "pride" and loved her son deeply, she would make comments like, "I know he ruined your life." She offered, at one point, to take a second mortgage on her home to help me buy one. Of course, I could not accept, but never forgot her generous offer.

When she died, I knew that I had to go back for the funeral and made the decision to honor her by accepting the invitation to also go to my ex's home afterwards. It was awkward and uncomfortable but my children were proud of me and I felt it was the right thing to do.

After I had been there for awhile, the ex approached me and asked if we could talk. He then proceeded to ask me to forgive him and stated that he knew what he did was wrong. I told him that I could forgive, but not forget. I wish I had also told him that it was not the suffering I had encountered, but that he had totally abandoned his duties and responsibilities as a father. That was the most unforgiveable. Having four children in college at the same time (one in professional school) could have been so much easier with his help.

He was looking for some atonement because he and his wife had a renewed religious fervor. He stated that they "were born again." Unfortunately, this increased his always inability to refrain from judging others. All of a sudden, he and his wife were "clean." His biggest judgmental attitude was towards his son who had recently come out as a gay person. I also wanted to scream, "Show me the money," a quote from a recent movie that I had seen.

CHAPTER TWENTY-ONE

The real estate market in Lexington during the early 1980s was terrible. Interest rates were 18 and 19 percent. With my meager connections and contacts, I simply could not pay my bills. In 1982, I had two older children still in college, with the two younger ones starting. I decided to take a property management course and try to get a job in the rental market. Luckily, I landed a job as an assistant manager at a property. Within the year, I was able to get a manager's position. This particular community was predominantly inhabited by college students who loved the party scene. Many days were spent trying to soothe ruffled feathers of students and parents who claimed to not understand our rules, especially those pertaining to parking. Daddies constantly wanted to sue me over their son or daughter realizing that their car had been towed, despite consistent warnings. After three years of feeling stressed and harassed with this job, I gave it up, going back into real estate and sporadic income. Needless to say, I was struggling.

Naiveté was also my middle name. This particular real estate office was full of very aggressive salespersons, who would swipe a client from right under your nose, without batting an eyelash. I used to think, "The barracudas are on attack," and knew if that was the secret to a lot of success in this business, I was doomed.

A former college friend was a housemother for a sorority on campus at the University of Kentucky. She told me about an opening at another house that would be available in the fall. I decided to apply through the Dean of Women's office on campus.

My mother had died. One child was in law school, one in medical school, one studying physical therapy, and the other one graduated from NYU. He was on his own in New York City, doing "off-Broadway," and trying to make it in the theatre world. The decision to take the housemother position ended up being one of the best in my life. Not only did I have so much fun with the girls and other housemothers, but I felt the most carefree that I had in years. I had no bills because everything was paid for. I had lots of free time, making new friends with a great group of other housemothers. I was even able, one summer, to go to Europe with my old western Kentucky girlfriends.

Soon, the idea struck. Why not take a couple of classes at the University? I was right on campus with no parking problems and had free time during the day. Besides, I had always been a bit ashamed of not having a degree. Probably some of my insecure fears coming to roost, remembering having been told, "I could never make it in the real world."

Okay, what to take? Well, I always had an artistic streak and loved decorating, working with textiles, colors, etc. I had an interview with the head of the Design Department. I expressed my desire, but also my misgivings, about being unable to draw much more than a stick person. He assured me that this was not a "have to" in order to be a designer. One of my first assignments was to sketch a building on campus. I have to tell you that when they put my work on the board, in that classroom with all of the others, I wanted to run as far away as I could and hide. So, I guess you could say that my short-lived designer career ended very abruptly.

Finally, I decided that in this period of my life, I wanted a career where I could "make a difference" with others. So, I enrolled in the College of Social Work. It seemed the right fit for this period of my life.

Petrified that I could not make it, being now in my fifties, I started taking only a couple of classes. I had to conquer biology and math undergraduate courses before I could get into the social work curriculum. Training my "old brain" to absorb and retain factual information was indeed a challenge. I had many moments of self-doubt, but persevered.

One of my first encounters with a professor in the College of Social Work had a profound effect. This very tall, older, and distinguished gentleman had a reputation for harassing and intimidating women students. Many of my colleagues, as well as myself, lived in terror that he would single us out for one of his frightening tirades.

Perhaps sensing and feeding on my insecurities, I became his target. After going home from class many days in tears, I decided enough was enough and I would not allow myself to be bullied or intimidated again. I arranged an appointment with Professor B and asked him not to speak until I had finished. Shaking with fear and trying not to show it,

I proceeded to assert some bravery into my tone of voice. I said, "Professor B, I want you to know that I respect you as a person and as a teacher. However, at this point in my life, I do not allow anyone to talk down to me." He was startled, but in a very kind voice, apologized. This particular teacher became one of my greatest advocates and ended up nominating me for several awards given by the college.

My children persuaded me to walk in cap and gown, threatening to hold up a sign that said "We finally got our mother out of school." When they called my name as the recipient of the "Outstanding Student in the College of Social Work" award, I was emotionally touched and honored. Looking into the audience and seeing my oldest son wiping away tears was a special moment in life. This award was voted on by the entire senior class of students, which made it even more important to me.

I also received the award for the outstanding student in the College, voted on by the faculty. This award, I feel, was spearheaded by my old adversary turned advocate, Professor B. This was a very proud time in my life. My older cousin from Florida had flown in for the occasion, my friend and cook from the sorority house presented me with roses, and the girls yelled, "Way to go, Mom." It was one of those moments in time not to be forgotten. This was the best thing I had ever accomplished for myself and it restored my self-esteem. I thought, at the time, that I could climb mountains! I was a college graduate at fifty-eight.

I continued into the master's program and because of my academic standing, was able to graduate in one and a half years. I received my MSW in August, after turning sixty the previous May. I was on my way to a social work career. One of my internships had been in a low-income senior housing setting and I had loved it. Not only did they make me feel young, but it was very satisfying work, finding needed resources to improve their quality of life. More important, was taking the time to listen to their feelings and emotions. Geriatric Social Work became a passionate, self-satisfying, and fulfilling career for me.

I had a purpose.

CHAPTER TWENTY-TWO

Never in my wildest dreams did I imagine that I would love public speaking. I became quite good at it and found myself doing workshops, seminars, etc., on many aging issues. One of my friends and colleague claimed that I became a different person when in front of an audience. I have to admit that I get a certain feeling of euphoria when speaking. Perhaps my childhood dreams of becoming a famous star were somehow being transformed in this small way.

I was also asked to teach in the College of Social Work at UK, as an adjunct professor, which allowed me to once again be involved with the student world. I am proud to say that I received recognition as "Teacher Who Made a Difference," while also receiving the "Field Instructor Award." All thanks to two special students. It may sound braggadocio to mention these accomplishments, but you have to remember from "whence I come." The fear, self-deprecating, and demoralizing attitudes were no more. A victory of sorts!

Occasionally, I must admit that I creep back into that painful abyss and self-flagellation, but have to remind myself of the journey and accomplishments that have come my way. I also have some very good friends to remind me to "straighten up" and be grateful. Also, I thank God for a sense of humor and the ability to laugh at myself.

The longer I live, the more I realize the impact of attitude on life. We cannot change our past and we cannot change the fact that people will act in a certain way. I am convinced that life is 10% what happens to me and 90% of how I react to it. The lesson of all this is that we are in charge of our attitudes. Life often gives us lemons, but with creativity, we can make sweet lemonade. Also, I realize that all of life's choices, whether good or bad, bring consequences.

I recently asked my daughter what she thought my life might be like if I had remained in that same town and in the big house. She answered quickly, "You would have not become nearly as interesting."

CHAPTER TWENTY-THREE

Looking back, I wish that I had met someone and had a loving relationship. I am sad that I will never know what that would be like. I know that it was just "not in the stars." I was so busy trying to make it in this world, plus I know that I was also afraid to trust. I admit to being damaged where the opposite sex was concerned and wish that I had sought therapy.

When I first moved to Lexington, my real estate friends would try to get me to go out in the evening with them to bars or couples gathering places. One friend exclaimed in desperation, "You never get out of the house! Do you think someone is coming down your chimney?" So, I said okay, and proceeded to go to the local "meet market," or should I say "meat market." Someone came from behind and tapped me on the shoulder. I nearly jumped out of my skin. That scene was not for me. I needed to be home with two teenage boys, who I felt needed that security of mom being available. Perhaps, I was too protective, but again, I felt guilty for bringing them to a totally new environment. I felt responsible for their happiness.

My boys could not have performed better in school. They were on the tennis team, speech team, Beta Club, school musical, Honor Society, and were even escorts for the local debutantes. So, in many ways, I was blessed.

CHAPTER TWENTY-FOUR

My son completed his law degree without any financial assistance from his father, even though it was in our divorce agreement that he be responsible. It was a struggle for my son to achieve this degree and thought it was fitting to file suit against his father, only he said, to make a statement and not try to collect. He said, "I want it on record that he did not live up to his agreement." I think when he did this, his anger seemed to diminish. So, it was perhaps a good thing. He had kept pent-up negative emotions for so long. Like my therapeutic writing of this story, this was an outlet for him to let go of that negative energy and move on with his life. After this incident, he seemed to be able to establish some sort of relationship with his father.

All of the children, although not close, want that relationship from their father. They simply want a little piece of him. He has not always been there for them, but has reached out more now that they are grown and successful. Of course, the wife comes first and always has. He had put all of his assets into her name early on in the game, to protect them from lawyers and courts. He recently told my oldest son that there would be no inheritance. No surprise there.

Last year, he was named Outstanding Alumni of his University Alma Mater and was Grand Marshall in the Homecoming Parade. He wanted all of his children there to bask in his glory and even paid for the son in California to come. He is still the respected Baby Doctor in the community. Most folks do not have a clue about him not fulfilling default obligations to his own children. He is still a prominent figure in the community. The elementary school is named after his father, for goodness sakes.

So, if anyone reads this from that town, they will probably be in shock or disbelief. I am sure that I am bursting a few bubbles! I have been told stories suggesting that I had affairs and also spent all of his money. So people believe what they want to believe. After all, he is the hometown boy and that has always carried a lot of weight within the community. I simply cannot worry about that!

Sorry, Church Ladies, you were wrong about the affairs. You gave me credit for a lot of fun I never had.

CHAPTER TWENTY-FIVE

I had spent all day at an aging conference and was anxious to get home. The first thing that I did when entering my home was to take off my shoes and bra. But, then I got the call. The caretakers from the Woman's Club of Central Kentucky were frantically telling me that there was a very unruly group renting the space and, because I was President, should come immediately. My first thought was to call the police but then decided to check it out first.

Needless to say, I was not happy to get in my car and drive from my home in Versailles to Lexington, after putting in a very tiring day.

When I pulled into the lot, I saw plenty of cars, but did not hear a big ruckus going on. As I entered the dining room, about forty-plus people jumped out, screaming "Happy Birthday!" There stood my children, grandchildren, brother, sister-in-law, and many friends. It was my seventy-fifth birthday. My daughter and granddaughter had planned this surprise. There were lots of presents, refreshments, and a big cake with a huge 75 on it, along with banners advertising this significant occasion. Never mind that I had avoided telling my age to friends and colleagues. I felt like I had been in the closet and this was my coming-out party. There is still a huge stigma in the workplace. Somehow, you become diminished because of your age. So, I had fallen into the "don't ask, don't tell" category. To this day, people say to me, "I did not know you were that old." I reply, "I don't feel that old."

My workplace buddies came up with the idea that I should properly celebrate this monumental occasion with a tattoo. The boss paid for it and I was accompanied by two of my colleagues to a tattoo parlor, close to the office.

I proceeded to get my ankle butterfly, celebrating that I am at age seventy-five feeling free, liberated, and content with who I am. It is indeed a conversation piece and I wear it with pride.

My teenage grandson said to his parents, "If Amie can get a tattoo, why can't I?"

My answer was, "When you get to 75, you can do just that."

CHAPTER TWENTY-SIX

It has been quite a journey. I now find myself, seventy-seven years old, still working part-time, in good health except for a pair of arthritic knees, and finding life both challenging and exhilarating. My three sons, a Doctor, Lawyer, and Indian Chief (Actor), and my beautiful daughter, a Physical Therapist, are doing well and have been successful. I have five wonderful grandchildren. The pain that I have suffered has subsided, and possibly has contributed to moral strengths helpful as one enters the aging process. I have finally forgiven and that is liberating.

This story could only happen at a certain time in history, when displaced homemakers with no thoughts of outside careers, learned to adapt to new lifestyles and acquire a new resilience to the struggles of making a living and surviving. It is also a discovery of self, knowing that the journey you take makes you the person you become, combined with feelings of sadness and loss of what could have been. In the 1970s and 1980s, the US underwent a "Divorce Revolution." Many women caught in this wave had devoted themselves to their husbands' personal and professional needs. Wives often assisted in putting their husbands through school, while sacrificing any thoughts of their own careers.

One of my closest friends had a horrific experience with the court system, in the same town, during the same time frame. She ended with very minimal support for her three children, with little equity in her home, and no job skills. She asked the judge how they could live. His answer was that she should move in with her mother. Her ex-husband was a college professor, dean of his department, and continued to have an adequate salary. She left town with $1,500 and some furniture. Friends let her live with them until she could find work. With only a high school education and suffering many setbacks, she eventually became one of the most successful furniture salespersons in a large city.

Many similar stories exist.

Women of that day often bought into "the social contract of man, the provider, and woman, the homemaker." Those were the days of watching the Cleavers on "Father Knows Best" and the perceived notion that marriages lasted forever. Enter the turbulent 1960s and 1970s, and some say, the "moral collapse" of our society. In the United States, the 1960s was also a period of great unrest and dramatic change. The "Sexual Revolution" was born. The ideas and philosophy of the 1960s became mainstream in the 1970s – sexual freedom, the legalization of abortion, birth control, etc.

In the late-1960s and 1970s, most states adopted the policy of "no-fault" divorce laws. This meant that either party in the marriage could sue for divorce with only the claim of "irreconcilable differences." Therefore, divorce was an "easy exit" in dealing with problems for couples. The result was marital disruption, which had detrimental economic effects on women and children. In the mid-1970s, it was said that more American marriages ended in divorce than in death. Retirement accounts, health coverage, etc., frequently went out the window. We often see the only source of retirement earnings to be social security. Retirement is a luxury that many will most likely not get to afford. Poverty is a real problem for many.

So this is part of the story…

I used to tell the children "All of these obstacles build character." I must tell you that I don't need any more character at this point in my life!

Maybe my story can lend itself to some awareness of the social phenomenon and financial plight, of the older divorced woman, that exists in our society. Perhaps we were born at the wrong time, as women of my day bought into the social contract that women were the homemakers and men were the providers. Regardless, there were many women who fit the "displaced homemaker" status and I don't think much has been written about it.

The definition of survival is to remain alive or in existence, to carry on despite hardships or trauma, persevere, remain functional or usable, to outlive others, and to cope.

My goal is that by writing "Starting Over," I have fulfilled that definition. Many other women of my time in history have experienced the same.

The journey continues, hopefully with understanding, love, perseverance, and resilience.

In some ways, I feel that I have not been very kind to my ex-husband, but then I realize that this is the hard and cold truth as I know it. After all, if one wants to be remembered warmly, they should have behaved differently. Or, as the old saying goes,

"What goes around, comes around."

After all, he is not the same person he was thirty-five years ago. Age has not been so kind. His young wife, however, just ran a triathlon and looks the best she ever has. So, the generation difference is profound and significant. Actually, it is rather a sad state of affairs.

Karma is a bitch!

My anger is no more. All of that negative energy is leaving me. Forgiveness has set me free.

I feel a sense of freedom and my spirit is renewed! Writing has been my therapy.

As this goes to print, I am launching a new business venture, a Geriatric Care service. The story has not ended and I am looking forward to the next chapter. The journey and challenges continue, and hopefully, the resilience and perseverance of the human soul compensates for what is to come.

Like the butterfly, life is full of transition, hope and change. I am finally able to spread my wings, connect with my spirit, and free my soul of any past bitterness.

Life is good!

PHOTOGRAPHS

Papa Bernard surrounded by grandchildren and great grandchildren.

Janice, age 5.

Daddy at work.

My beautiful Mother.

My brother, Mother and me.

Cheerleader at Louisville Manual High School
age 16.

My wedding day.

Me with my four children in Ft. Hood, Texas.

Janice age 35, living in the big house!

"We finally got our Mother out of school" 1994

Me today! Butterfly status?

ABOUT THE AUTHOR

Janice Austin has a BSW and MSW from the University of Kentucky and has been a Geriatric Social Worker for twenty years. She is very proud of her four children and five grandchildren, loves to go shopping, junking and out to lunch with her special friends. She is currently President of the Woman's Club of Central Kentucky, the oldest woman's club in the country. for the second time and has served on many community boards and committees.

Made in the USA
Charleston, SC
16 August 2014